Becoming A Skilled Spiritual Supporter

The Helping Relationship Series

Pastor Amy Halas Goff, MS

DEDICATION

For those who seek their joy;
And to those who have found it and share.

CONTENTS

	Acknowledgments	i
1	Introduction	3
2	Scope, Safety, and the Law	8
3	Boundaries and Referring	14
4	Biblical Basics	21
5	Psychological Basics	31
6	Skilled Spiritual Supporter Model, Stage I, Identification	42
7	Skilled Spiritual Supporter Model, Stage II, Evaluation	49
8	Skilled Spiritual Supporter Model, Stage III, Implementation	55
9	Skilled Spiritual Supporter Model, Stage IV, Follow-up	61
10	Final Notes	64

ACKNOWLEDGMENTS

I would like to thank those who have taken part in this course, with thanks for their invaluable feedback and love for Helping.

INTRODUCTION

The Bible talks about helping and helping relationships in many different ways. In his letter to the Philippians Paul wrote, "Let each of you look not only to his own interests, but also to the interests of others" (Philippians 2:4).

A Skilled Spiritual Support uses the scriptures and science to bring clients a Godly sense of Security, Significance, and Identity; thereby, facilitating lasting, positive, Godly change while empowering the client's ability to help themselves. A Skilled Spiritual Supporter is one who demonstrates Christ-like unconditional positive regard in their helping relationship.

There are many terms and ideas that I present, but there are two main definitions that will help you throughout this text. Although there are several definitions for both of these constructs depending on the field of study, for our purposes here, I will use the following definitions for *biblical counseling* and *psychology*.

Biblical Counselor:

Biblical counseling is one of many types of helping relationships. The significance here is the emphasis on lining up the client's needs with God's will for their life.

A biblical counselor is one who emphasizes the use of spiritual resources, such as scriptures and prayer, as well as using traditional counseling methods, to guide a client through the process of identifying and mediating their concerns. "All Scripture is breathed out by God and profitable for teaching, for reproof, for correction, and for training righteousness, that the man of God may be complete, equipped for every good work" (2Timothy 3:16-17).

Psychology:

Psychology is the science of human behaviors and cognitions in response to life circumstances. Psychology explains that there are response mechanisms that apply to distress, crisis, and other issues. This may be an over-simplified definition; however, it is the kernel of truth. Psychology is still a relatively young discipline with new research and developments being published often.

Helping relationships can be complicated and multi-layered. The most important aspect of any helping relationship is attention to safety. The client's safety and your own.

The Skilled Spiritual Supporter Model is a flow chart and paradigm for bringing a knowledgeable skillset to each helping relationship. In this text we will detail and explain each stage.

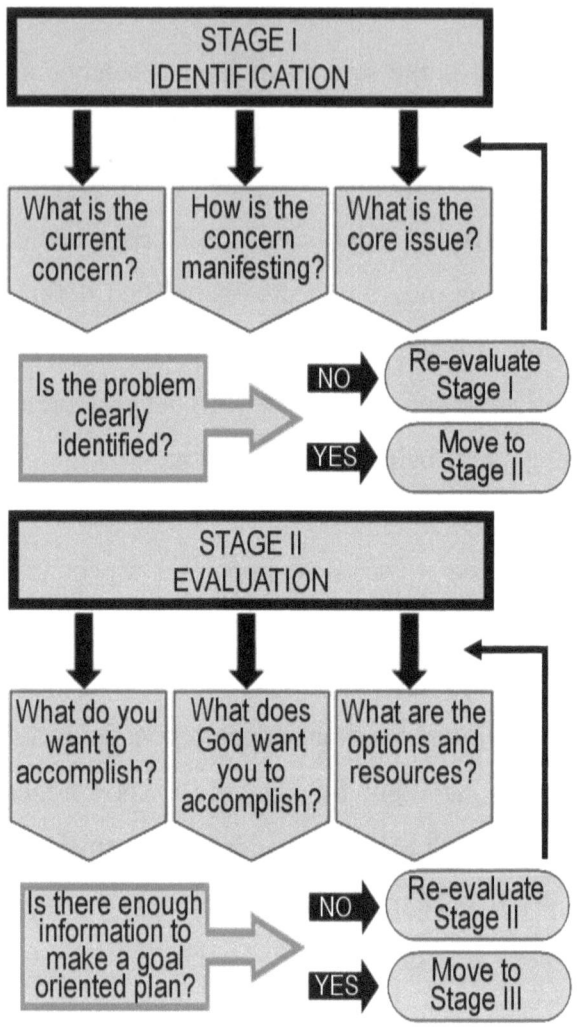

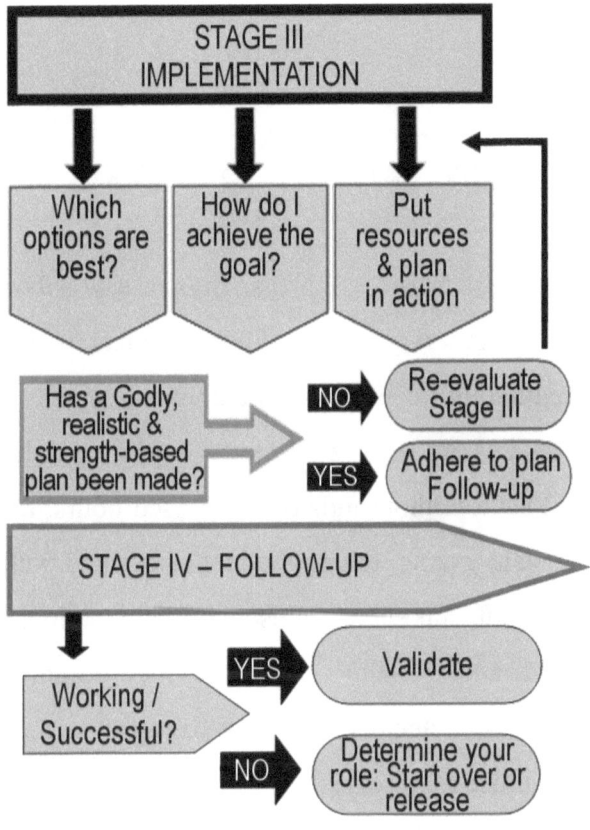

2 SCOPE, SAFETY, AND THE LAW

The scope of Skilled Spiritual Supporters is both very broad and very narrow. Each state has its own laws regulating licensure for therapists. Typically, a therapist has at least a master's degree and has accrued several thousands of supervised hours, and passed state exams. Because client safety and well-being are at stake the industry is very seriously regulated and penalties are stiff for promoting yourself, even accidently, as a therapist without meeting those requirements.

Be mindful that without a state license it is out of your scope to provide therapy or counseling. You are providing skilled help. Pastoral counseling is another helping relationship with specific boundaries. Pastoral counseling can only be conducted by a professionally certified religious leader such as minister, priest, rabbi, imam, etc. These leaders are typically trained not only in their religious traditions but also in psychological constructs which allow them to use a psychospiritual model. There are legal boundaries regarding the limits of pastoral counseling. You must be cautious to not overstate your religious training.

Finally, we come to skilled helping. As we already touched upon, a skilled spiritual helper is one who has a basic understanding of biblical and psychological principles and uses that knowledge to compassionately guide a client through a Godly path of decision making and personal accountability.

There are legal restrictions related to therapeutic support and helping relationships. These laws and regulations are designed to protect the consumer from malpractice. Being compliant with state and federal laws also protects the helper. As a

Skilled Spiritual Supporter it is out of your scope to offer diagnostic opinions, or attempt therapy of any type. It *is* within your scope to suggest a higher level of support. In fact it is ethically vital that you do so. This is not to designed to undermine your importance. Many people simply need guidance and support, not medical or psychological intervention. You have an important role, just be clear you are not trying to do the job God assigned someone else:

"Only let each person live the life the Lord has assigned him and live it in the condition he was in when God called him. This is the rule I lay down in all the congregations" (1 Corinthians 7:17).

There are three main points to cover in this chapter: Legal Boundaries, Mandated Reporting, and Ethics Codes.

Legal Considerations. Each state board, for example the California Board of Behavioral Sciences, is very specific in defining the roles of licensed therapists, social workers, counselors, psychologists, and pastoral counselors. While these definitions and licensure requirements may vary by state, the concept remains intact, that is, you legally cannot promote yourself or operate as if you have a skill set that is not supported by your education or licensure. Offering support within your scope is a safety issue as well as a legal one. Your client may require interventions that you are not academically or legally capable of offering. Further, attempting to help outside of your scope can be deleterious to you on an emotional and spiritual level.

Mandated Reporting and Safety. I absolutely cannot state emphatically enough how vital addressing safety is. You may hear things in your helping relationship that require specific safety measures. You need to be aware of your client's safety, for example someone talking about suicide needs immediate intervention, do not take it upon yourself to determine the seriousness of their intent.

Of particular concern is the safety of children and the elderly—those who are the most vulnerable to abuse. Mandated reporters must legally report suspicions of abuse or face legal action, despite any premise of confidentiality. According to

Childwelfare.gov "While some States require all people to report their concerns, many States identify specific professionals as mandated reporters; these often include social workers, medical and mental health professionals, teachers, and child care providers. Specific procedures are usually established for mandated reporters to make referrals to child protective services." Similarly, all states have laws pertaining to reporting elder abuse, they vary by state.

The United States Department of Health and Human Services provides links related to child maltreatment and elder abuse; hhs.gov

Ethics Codes. Simply stated ethics are the concepts we use to define our moral actions. Ethics help us decide which behaviors are right or wrong. Ethical principles can be found in personal behaviors, professional behaviors, and cultural behaviors. Ethics can be difficult to navigate, there are times when we encounter grey areas, that is to say, areas or circumstances that may cause moral dilemmas. In the helping professions, ethical codes of conduct are clearly written out.

Links to Ethics Codes:

Bible; Exodus 20:1-17

American Psychological Association; apa.org

American Association of Christian Counselors; aacc.net

National Christian Counselors Association; ncca.org

The goal of all ethics codes is to exemplify and demonstrate beneficence (doing good to others) vs. the absence of malfeasance (doing harm to others). The Bible provides us with the Ten Commandments and with examples of ethical conduct throughout Proverbs and in parables. Legally binding ethics codes have been established by organizations of prominence in the helping professions. These codes detail standards for the conduct expected of practitioners; they are powerful tools for understanding boundaries and behaviors.

3 BOUNDARIES AND REFERRING

There are limits to helping. As with many social situations there are appropriate times and places for offering skilled spiritual support. There are also appropriate times to decline helping. In western culture we identify our boundaries to be respectful of each other and of ourselves. Boundaries help us explain our responsibilities and our expectations of each other. The boundaries you set as a Skilled Spiritual Supporter will enable your client to individuate from you. In a helping relationship boundary questions include: "When do I help?" "How do I help?" and "What are my limits?"

These questions have a few obvious answers.

When do I help?

When To Help	"Therefore let us draw near with confidence to the throne of grace, so that we may receive mercy and find grace to help in time of need." Hebrews 4:16
• When asked ➡ • With permission	

If Someone asks you for help and it is reasonable to do so, help! If you see a need that is in your scope and conscience to help, offer! Hebrews 4:16 states, "Therefore let us draw near with confidence to the throne of grace, so that we may receive mercy and find grace to help in time of need." However, we must be cautious to not over step boundaries by trying to help when assistance is unwelcome or unwanted.

How do I help?

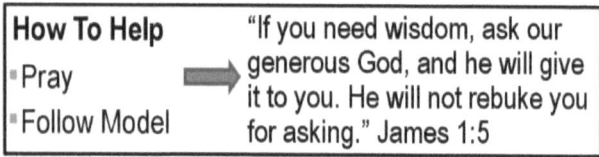

Most importantly be prayerful at every stage; you will need God and you will be modeling dependence upon God. We should pray for wisdom: "If you need wisdom, ask our generous God, and he will give it to you. He will not rebuke you for asking" James 1:5. Then, follow the stages of the Skilled Spiritual Supporter Model. It provides a template for the rest of the process.

Finally, *know your limits.*

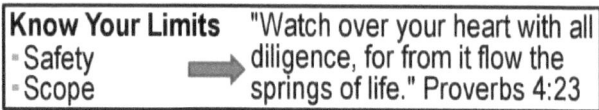

Make sure you are safe and your client is safe. Be careful that the help you offer is legally and ethically appropriate for you.

Lastly, occasionally over the course of your helping relationship you may find that you are uncomfortable for some reason. Listen to the discernment the Lord gives you. At *no time* should you force yourself into a helping situation that makes you concerned about your spiritual, physical, or emotional safety. "Watch over your heart with all diligence, for from it flow the springs of life" (Proverbs 4:23).

More on boundaries. Don't work harder than your client at resolving the issues. There are psychological reasons for this including the concepts of 'buy-in' and accountability. If someone is not making their own effort they are not taking responsibility for their concerns and therefore not taking responsibility for their solutions. This lack of personal accountability is a set-up for failure. You simply cannot follow them around and resolve their issues for them forever. Your goal is to help them to help themselves. Paul brought this point home in his letter to the Galatians, "Do your own work well, and then you will have something to be proud of.

But don't compare yourself with others. We each must carry our own load" (Galatians 6:4-5).

There are several reasons why we may need to refer our clients to a different level of helper. Safety first and foremost. Does your client require medical care? Refer. Is your client mentally ill? Refer. Does your client have spiritual needs beyond your capability? Refer. Are you unable to see the process though for any reason? Refer.

"We have different gifts, according to the grace given to each of us." Romans 12:6

We each have our gifts or training or ministry. We don't need to feel so responsible to our clients that we stretch out of our legal or ethical boundaries. If you know your own limitations and boundaries, then knowing when to refer is basic. There are things we simply cannot handle on our own as Skilled Spiritual Supporters. Romans 12:3 reminds us that "For by the grace given me I say to every one of you: Do not think of yourself more highly than you ought, but rather think of yourself with sober judgment, in accordance with the faith God has distributed to each of you." It is not just important but vital that you give yourself the mercy to realize when your client would benefit from a different skilled or professional supporter. As an example, if someone seeking your help is struggling with addiction consider referring to a licensed drug and alcohol provider; addiction dynamics are specific and potentially very dangerous. Further, if someone is facing a serious mental illness it is not in a Skilled Spiritual Supporter's scope to offer diagnosis or treatment. We can offer prayer, certainly! We may also choose to offer a list of options such as contact information for more appropriate, long term helpers. And lastly, our personal lives can get complicated, make sure you have a back-up plan and back-up Skilled Supporter for your client in the event of your own illness, emergency, etc.

A special note on addiction. Physical and behavioral addictions are incredibly complex and potentially life-threatening issues. As a Skilled Spiritual Supporter you are not equipped to solely meet the needs of an addicted client. SAFETY MUST COME FIRST. Your role with the addicted client should be limited to assistance in referral and resource location, and possibly as an accountability partner.

These internet resources are for the most common addictions:

- *Alcoholics Anonymous:* aa.org

- *Eating Disorders Anonymous:* eatingdisordersanonymous.org

- *Gamblers Anonymous*: gamblersanonymous.org

- *Internet & Tech Addiction Anonymous:* netaddictionanon.org

- *Narcotics Anonymous:* na.org

- *Porn Addicts Anonymous:* pornaddictsanonymous.org

- *Sex Addicts Anonymous:* saa-recovery.org

- *Shopaholics Anonymous:* shopaholicsanonymous.org

4 BIBLICAL BASICS

There are seven definitions to remember in this chapter. While alternate definitions may be available elsewhere, this text presents operational definitions as they apply to the biblical concepts presented here:

Theocentric; Theocentricity is literally God-centered dynamics. The scriptures tell us of God's omnipotence. "For ever since the world was created, people have seen the earth and sky. Through everything God made, they can clearly see his invisible qualities—his eternal power and divine nature. So they have no excuse for not knowing God" (Romans 1:20). In this helping model we presume that nothing can be accomplished without God's direction.

First and foremost, biblical support should adhere to a theocentric methodology. That means the helping approach is God-centered and solution-based. Ephesians 4:6 reminds us that "There is one God and Father of everything. He rules everything and is everywhere and is in everything."

THEOCENTRIC METHODOLOGY:

► **God-centered**
► **Solution-focused**

When our life has God in the center our thoughts and behaviors will reflect His love and His will for us. To be genuinely God-Centered, helping methods must include frank discussions that include prayer, and scripture.

Security, Significance, and Identity are interconnected concepts of personal well-being.

Security is how safe we feel. Feelings of security mean we have good attachments and healthy trust and dependence with no fear of abandonment. When we do not feel secure in our relationships we can turn to unhealthy relationships and live with skewed boundaries.

God promised us that He can give us security!

Security ➞	"...but now I will heal and mend
▪ Attachment	them. I will make them whole and
▪ Trust	bless them with an abundance of
▪ Dependence	peace and security." Jeremiah 33:6

Significance is how we believe others see us. We can suffer if our healthy ego does not believe we are respected or worthy. An excellent focus here is to remember that although we may not see ourselves as worthy or valuable, our significance to God is unfathomable.

Significance ▪ Respect ▪ Worth ▪ Ego	"I no longer call you servants, because a servant does not know his master's business. Instead, I have called you friends, for everything that I learned from my father I have made know to you." John 15:15

Our **Identity** is very personal. Identity is how we see ourselves, meaning our purpose and our role and even our boundaries. In a theocentric model we also believe that our identity should be who God sees when He sees us. Our identity should be shaped by who God says we are.

Identity ▪ Purpose ▪ Role	"Before I formed you in the womb I knew you, before you were born I set you apart, I appointed you as a prophet to the nations." Jeremiah 1:5

Distress, Crisis and Conflict are three main types of issues requiring skilled help. Many other issues exist, of course, but most could fall into one of these categories.

Distress is emotional turmoil that can be characterized by combinations of anxiety, anger, fear, pain, grief, or suffering. Distress can have a sudden onset or be chronic. Someone in distress is troubled. We need to remind them they are not alone in their pain and that the Lord hears them. Validating them is crucial.

Distress ⟹   "Out of distress I called on the
- Turmoil   Lord; the Lord answered me
- Mixed Symptoms   and set me free." Psalm 118:5

A **Crisis** is typically caused by some type of catastrophic event or circumstance creating extreme anguish or distress that requires an urgent response. A crisis may feel insurmountable and be characterized by feelings of hopelessness. Our aim is to help our clients know that God hears them.

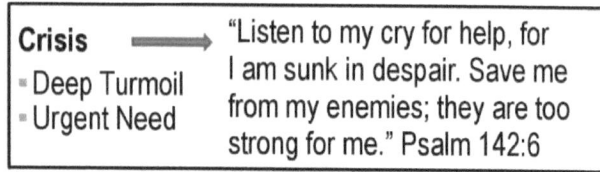

Conflict is an incompatibility of ideas, decisions, goals, or feelings. Conflict can be found between people and also within an individual. God has given us direction in conflict with others.

Conflict
- Turmoil
- Incompatibility

"Let all bitterness and wrath and anger and clamor and slander be put away from you, along with all malice." Ephesians 4:31

Romans 7:19 speaks to internal conflict, the author writes "I don't do the good that I want to do, but I do the evil that I don't want to do." God has given us ways out of this pain.

We know that bad things can happen to good people, and that they may need support to get to over some hurdle life has thrown them. But sometimes our issues or *distress* or *crisis* are the result of being out of alignment with God. In any event our primary goal as Skilled Spiritual Supporters is to help our clients regain their sense of *Security, Significance, and Identity*, with God, themselves, and within their other relationships.

> "Trust the Lord completely, and don't depend on your own knowledge. With every step you take, think about what He wants, and He will help you go the right way." Proverbs 3:5-6

As a Skilled Spiritual Supporter you must remember to use prayer, scripture, ethics, and accountability in your sessions. As a Christian you are already familiar with using these elements as part of your life as your testimony. In a helping relationship however, you need to remember that you are modeling Godly behaviors to someone who may not be using these elements in the most Christ-like way possible.

Prayer is the best way to begin and end each session. Your client hears you seeking God's direction and thanking Him for the changes you are working on together.

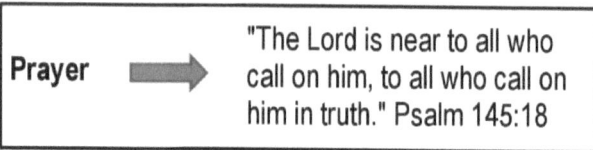

Using **scriptures** throughout your sessions helps to reinforce that you are modeling change on biblically sound principles. It lets your client know that you are doing more than offering your opinion. Scriptures can serve as homework assignments and sources of meditative focus.

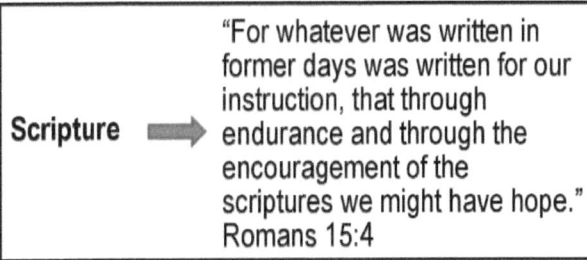

Ethics are a very important concept. Be mindful that you are operating A) from a place of Christ-like unconditional positive regard,

B) within the law, and C) within your scope.

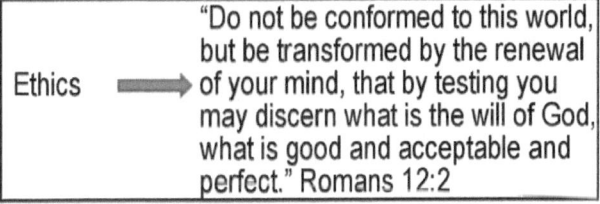

Finally, don't dismiss the importance of **accountability**. You are accountable to God for how you guide your client through this model. They are trusting you with their deep concerns. You are accountable not just for keeping you both safe, but also to God for how you represent the Bible and yourself to a vulnerable person.

It may benefit you to have an accountability partner that can be in prayer for you as a Skilled Spiritual Supporter without breaching confidentiality.

Accountability

"So then each of us will give an account of himself to God." Romans 14:12

"Iron sharpens iron, and one man sharpens another." Proverbs 27:17

5 PSYCHOLOGICAL BASICS

One way of referring to mental health issues that can be caused or exacerbated by crisis and distress is *pathology*.

Pathology:
1: the study of diseases and especially of the changes in the body produced by them
2: something abnormal; *especially*: the disorders in structure and function that occur in a particular disease
Merriam-Webster at http://www.wordcentral.com

Some psychological pathologies can be severe, and out of your scope as a Skilled Spiritual Supporter. For example schizophrenia, bi-polar disorder, and addictions, absolutely require a very high level of professional care. That being said, some pathologies can be mild and well within your skill set, for example confusion regarding career development, grief, or situational depression. In this model, pathologies are those constructs which are out of the client's norm and disordering the client's well-being. Simply put, a pathological condition is disruptive to the client's sense of security, significance, identity, or any combination of the three.

The Bible has a lot to tell us about emotional and psychological pathologies. Among the most important messages from the scriptures regarding pathological disruption, is that God cares about our turmoil and can make us whole!

> "When the righteous cry for help, the Lord hears and delivers them out of all their troubles. The Lord is near to the brokenhearted and saves the crushed in spirit. Many are the afflictions of the righteous, but the Lord delivers him out of them all. He keeps all his bones; not one of them is broken." Psalm 34:17-20

> "No temptation has overtaken you that is not common to man. God is faithful, and he will not let you be tempted beyond your ability, but with the temptation he will also provide the way of escape, that you may be able to endure it." 1 Corinthians 10:13

> "And after you have suffered a little while, the God of all grace, who has called you to his eternal glory in Christ, will himself restore, confirm, strengthen, and establish you." 1Peter 5:1

> "He restores my soul. He leads me in paths of righteousness for his name's sake." Psalm 23:3

We understand pathologies in the Bible by scriptural descriptions. For example Job, Jonah, King David, King Saul and the prophet Jeremiah all suffered from depression; Elijah was suicidal.

> "When David and his men reached Ziklag, they found it destroyed by fire and their wives and sons and daughters taken captive. So David and his men wept aloud until they had no strength left to weep." 1 Samuel 30:3-4

> "He (Elijah) came to a broom bush, sat down under it and prayed that he might die. "I have had enough, LORD," he said. "Take my life; I am no better than my ancestors." Then he lay down under the bush and fell asleep." 1 Kings 19:4-5

Paul wrote about bullying:

> "For when we came into Macedonia, we had no rest, but we were harassed at every turn-conflicts on the outside, fears within. But God, who comforts the downcast, comforted us by the coming of Titus, and not only by his coming but also by the comfort you had given him." 2 Corinthians 7:5-7

Even marital problems were not unheard of in ancient times:

> "Better is a dry morsel with quiet than a house full of feasting with strife." Proverbs 17:1

There are many more examples in the Bible of people just like you and me, people experiencing the same issues as you and me! I challenge you to find them and familiarize yourself with them for the benefit of your clients. The Bible is full of examples of people facing the same dilemmas and heartaches we face today.

~ Elijah was suicidal (1 Kings 19:4)

~ Naomi was a widow (Ruth)

~ Job went bankrupt (Job 1:21)

~ Peter denied Christ (Mark 14)

~ Martha worried about everything (Luke 10)

~ The Samaritan woman was divorced more than once (John 4)

~ Paul was too religious (1 Timothy 1)

~ Noah was a drunk (Gen 9:21)

~ Jacob was a liar (Gen 27)

~ Leah was not attractive (Gen 29)

~ Joseph was abused (Gen37)

~ Moses had a stuttering problem (Exodus 4:10)

~ Gideon was afraid (Judges 6)

~ Rahab was a prostitute (Joshua 2)

~ David was an adulterer & murderer (2 Samuel 11)

The Bible gives us examples of anxiety and anger as triggers for distress. It is no surprise that brave people are put in trying circumstances. The key is to look at options for solutions remembering that God "will hear and help."

> **"And Jehoshaphat feared, and set himself to seek the Lord, and proclaimed a fast throughout all Judah. And Judah gathered themselves together to ask help of the Lord; even out of all the cities of Judah they came to seek the Lord...'If, when evil cometh upon us, as the sword, judgment, or pestilence, or famine, we stand before this house and in Thy presence (for Thy name is in this house), and cry unto Thee in our affliction, then Thou wilt hear and help... O our God, wilt Thou not judge them? For we have no might against this great company that cometh against us, neither know we what to do; but our eyes are upon Thee." 2 Chroncles20:5-13**

The scriptures also give us some solution oriented constructs.

> **"A fool gives full vent to his spirit, but a wise man quietly holds it back." Proverbs 29:11**
>
> **"If your brother sins against you, go and tell him what he did wrong. Do this in private. If he listens to you, then you have helped him to be your brother again." Matthew 18:15**
>
> **What is causing all the quarrels and fights among you? Isn't it your desires battling inside you? You desire things and don't have them. You kill, and you are jealous, and you still can't get them. So you fight and quarrel. The reason you don't have is that you don't pray! Or you pray and don't receive, because you pray with the wrong motive, that of wanting to indulge your own desires." James 4:1-3**

However, we must be cognizant of safety. Discernment is important here. For example, if we are aware someone is in danger, staying silent is the foolish path. Likewise, going alone to confront a potentially volatile person could be foolish. We must use and encourage good judgment and apply the scriptures contextually and prayerfully.

The Bible speaks about internal conflict:

> **"I don't do the good that I want to do, but I do the evil that I don't want to do." Romans 7:19**
>
> **"Enthusiasm without knowledge is not good.**
> **If you act too quickly, you might make a mistake." Proverbs 19:2**

Most of our internal conflicts come down to one of two things: 1. Doing things we know to be wrong, or 2. Facing a decision that could be positive or negative. In both of these instances God uses the Bible to reassure us that we are not alone in those types of dilemmas! Validate your client as he or she works to define the issue. Things to help your client consider are: facing all the facts, exploring all the options, and assessing the value of outcomes.

We know the ramifications of living with conflict, crisis and distress: we just don't feel good. We may feel out of control, scared, or helpless. It is important to understand the physical and psychological events that our bodies go through when faced with distress, conflict, or crises. Any of these three constructs trigger what are called Stress Responses. Stressors trigger chemical reactions in the brain. The chemical reactions produced by neurotransmitters create three different types of responses: emotional, physical, and cognitive. While Stress Responses are exceedingly complex, here we look at a greatly oversimplified view of the mechanisms.

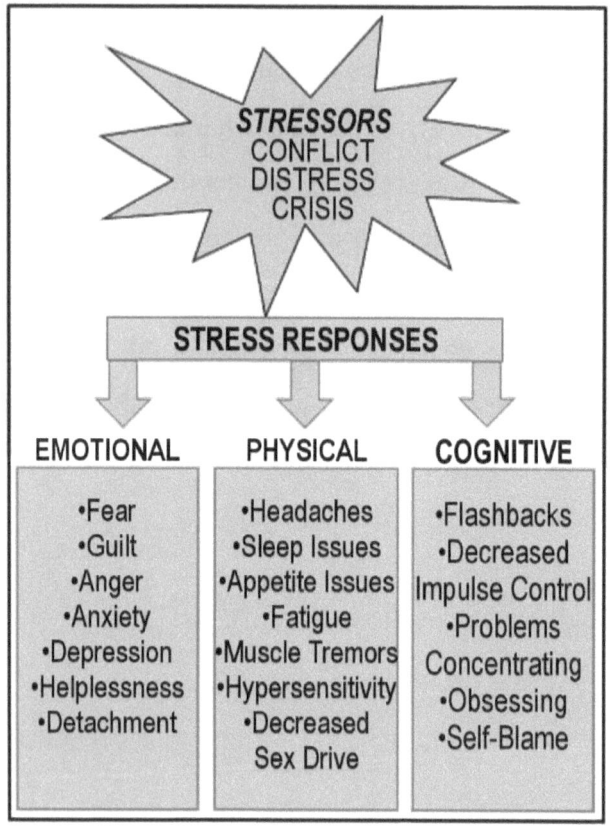

An important note here is that eustress; that is to say positive stressors, such as weddings and promotions, trigger the same physiological responses as distress, that is, negative stressors like divorce, or unemployment. It is important to validate any of these symptoms that your client may be experiencing. Remind them that those symptoms are common to their distress. However, be mindful that certain symptoms or severity of symptoms may indicate that your client's needs may be out of your scope and require a referral.

As you begin building a helping relationship with your client, remember that one of the most important things you can do for him or her is validate them. Whatever they are facing, it is a very real process for them. Your client needs your reassurance that God has not forgotten them, that they are not alone, and that there are remedies.

"And we know that all things work together for good to them that love God, to them who are called according to His purpose." Romans 8:28

Validating your client will go a long way toward building your client's trust and confidence in the problem solving process.

6 SKILLED SPIRITUAL SUPPORTER MODEL STAGE I, IDENTIFICATION

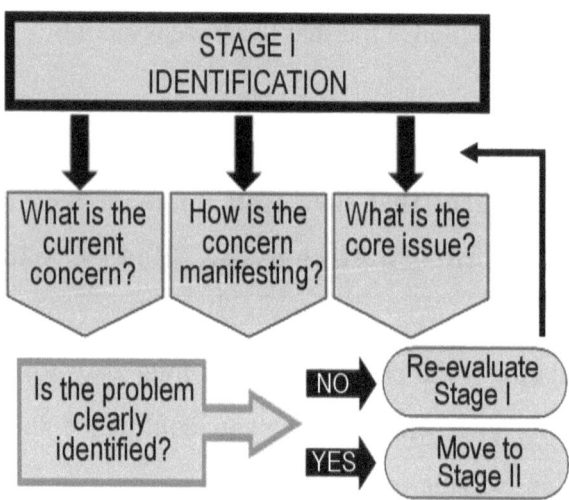

Stage One of the Skilled Spiritual Helper Model is fairly intuitive. Help your client specifically identify their problem.

What is your client's current concern? I strongly urge you to begin this first step with your client in prayer. Remember you are modeling your request for God's wisdom and guidance. What are they telling you? How are they telling you?

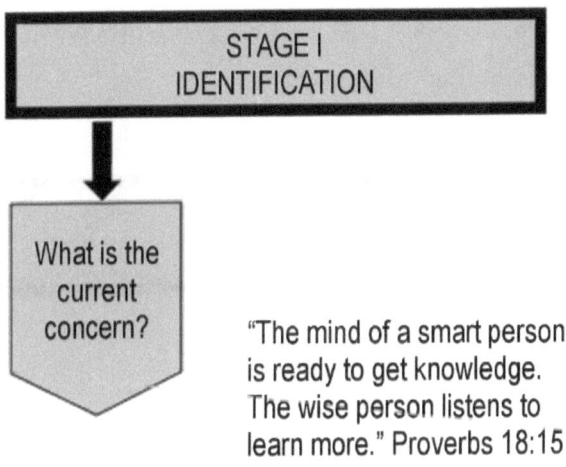

STAGE I
IDENTIFICATION

What is the current concern?

"The mind of a smart person is ready to get knowledge. The wise person listens to learn more." Proverbs 18:15

Step One is giving the client the opportunity to simply tell you their story, in their own words, in their own timing. A client may share with you a list of concerns or issues. Your role in Stage One is to help them narrow their focus by helping them to look at their concerns clearly. This may be difficult for them if several things are at play at the same time. Remember safety comes first. If you are hearing issues of abuse or neglect you must follow legal avenues! Again, the first thing you offer your client is your empathetic listening; this may be the first time they have had the chance to just talk things out. The next step is identifying the pathology, that is, the, 'symptoms' or 'manifestations' of the issues.

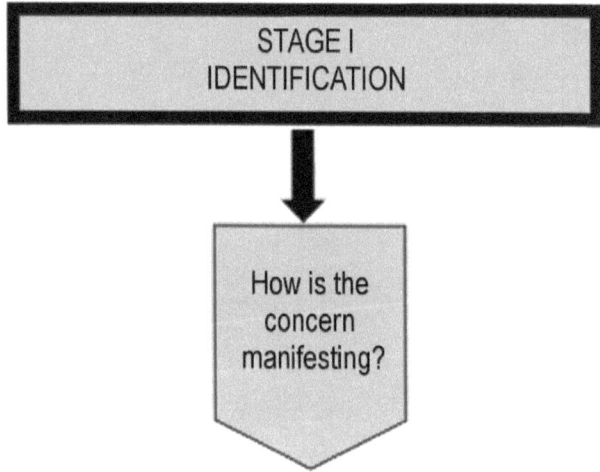

The way a problem manifests can sometimes assist you in helping your client identify the core issue or priority. For example, if the manifestation is that there is no food, the core issue is securing access to food supplies! On the other hand, your client may be reporting symptoms like sleep disturbances, moodiness, self-medicating, crying, etc. Some symptoms can seriously, negatively impact their daily functioning. In that event, you may need to consider referring to a higher skilled helper.

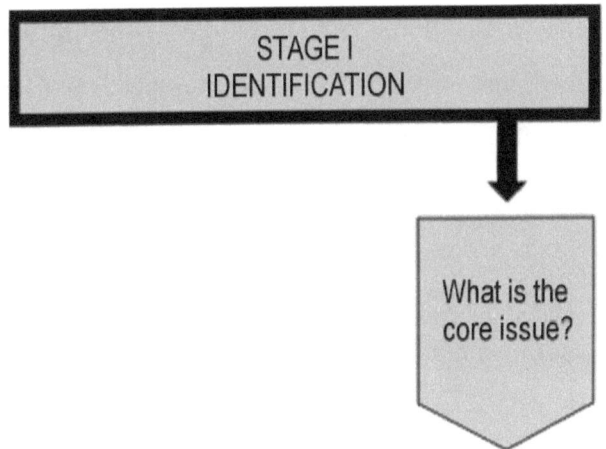

The hope is that by listening to your client's story and evaluating their manifestations of stress responses, you will be able to identify the core issue. It is vital that you guide your client into identifying that for themselves. This concept goes back to the topic of buy-in. Your function is to serve as a facilitator for your client to work the problem-solving steps for himself or herself. Consider this scenario: Your client, Jane, a single mom, comes to you complaining that she is miserable all the time, that her life is drudgery. Using Stage One, you ask her to tell you more about what is going on. As she tells you her story she reveals some of the manifestations of her misery: she becomes depressed and short tempered with her kids at the end of every weekend. She goes on to say she has started being late to work because the mornings are so hard for her, she calls in sick just so she won't have to go in, she leaves as early as she can because they don't appreciate her. You may ask probing questions to determine what other aspects of her life may be contributing to her misery. Such as 'how are your kids?' 'What are you doing for fun?' In this scenario, the client becomes animated and happy while talking about her great kids, and the adventures they have with friends and family.

Eventually you are able to determine that the core issue is job dissatisfaction. When your client is able to state, "My problem is that I need a new job," you have achieved Stage One and you can move on to help her identify the options or resources available to her to find a new job. Or find ways to accept her circumstances.

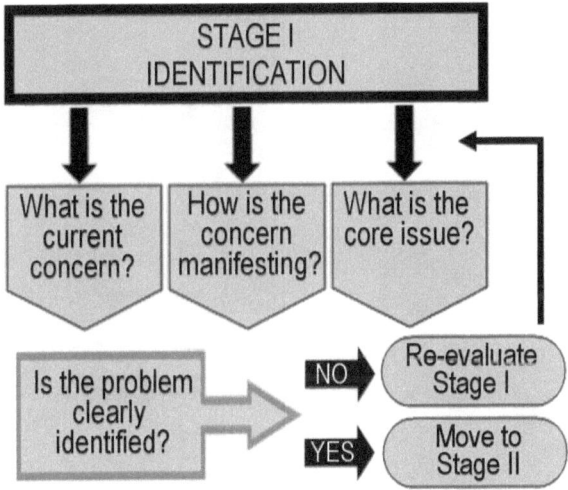

Ultimately, you help them evaluate if the problem is clearly defined and if you are able to help them move onto Stage II, or if the need to back up and redefine the core issue.

You may discover at the end of Stage One that some clients merely needed someone to bear witness to their pain, dilemma, or viewpoint. They may feel resolved simply because you took the time to validate them. They may also feel resolved because they were able to change their perspectives while talking things out. If that is the case, celebrate their success with them by thanking God; you are still modeling!

7 SKILLED SPIRITUAL SUPPORTER MODEL STAGE II, EVALUATION

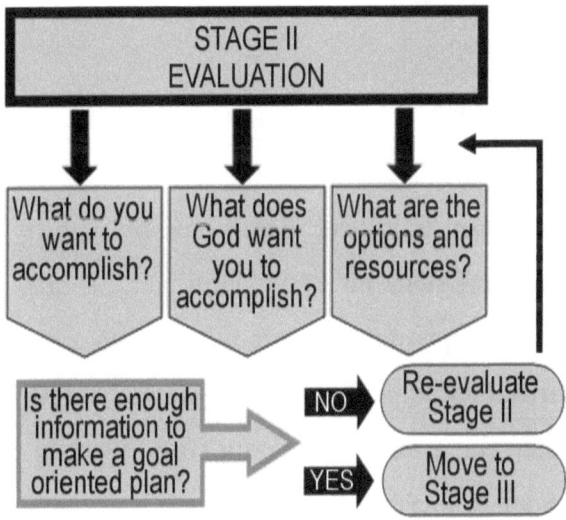

Stage Two of the Skilled Spiritual Helper Model is really where the client has the most work to do.

This stage requires from them a commitment to the process of resolving their issues, and a commitment to being honest with themselves about what they are really willing to do to accomplish their goals.

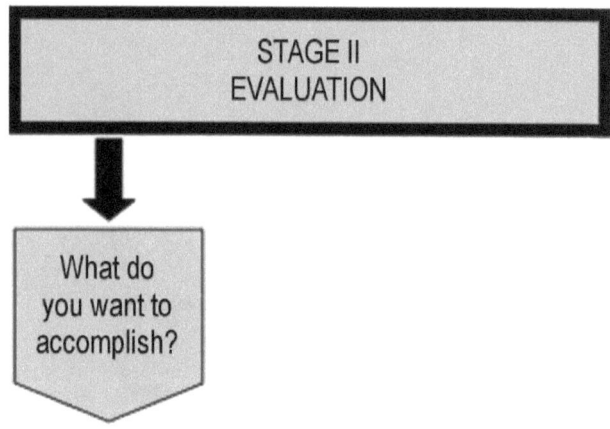

This question is basically answered by identifying the core problem or issue. However, it may be complex to answer. For example in our previous scenario, Jane identified that she wanted a new job. Someone in a similar situation may identify that they want to increase job satisfaction by being more involved or interacting more with co-workers outside of the office. As I keep reminding you, the key is to help the client identify what she or he sees as the goal.

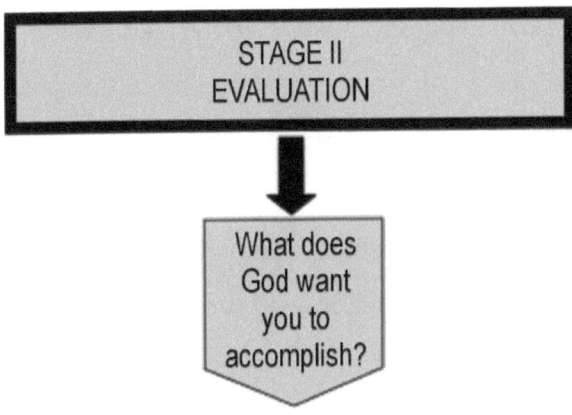

"A man's mind plans his way, but the Lord directs his steps and makes them sure." Proverbs 16:9

As a Skilled Spiritual Supporter, we are always looking for opportunities to reinforce God's will, God's Timing, God's Love, and God's purpose for our lives. When our lives are out of alignment with God's plan for us, the consequences can manifest in many ways. This can include the symptoms we discussed. Many times we can alleviate our cognitive and emotional discomfort by bringing our lives back in line with what we already know is God's will for us. There are times, though, when your client doesn't know God's plan for his life. This step is the most vital in the entire process. Because just as the scriptures tell us, we may make our plans, but only the Lord sustains the journey and outcome! Helping your client answer this question will entail prayer, scriptural support and discernment from you both.

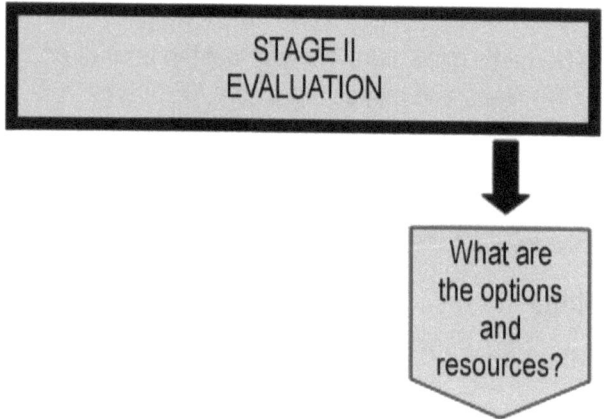

STAGE II
EVALUATION

What are the options and resources?

This is the time to lead your client in a brainstorming session. Encourage him or her to start by listing their personal strengths, then list their supporters, and assist them in listing resources that may be available in the community (church, public transportation, food banks, etc.). This reminds them that they are capable of change, and they are not alone in their change. Next help him or her to list all the options they can think of, include some of your own if they slow down. Be cautious of your role. Your client my see you as a resource for more than the problem solving process. Be personally mindful of how involved you want to be or how appropriate such involvement is. Remember, you are trying to facilitate self-sufficiency. Back to our example, Jane. She may list her degree in computers as a personal strength and she may list her parents as supporters. Under job search resources she may list online websites, local job fairs, and local career centers.

A lot has been written about the importance of the psychology of hope. This step gives your client the ability to hope for something better and examine all the possible ways to achieve it.

Your goal here is to help facilitate viable and valid possibilities for a God-centered future.

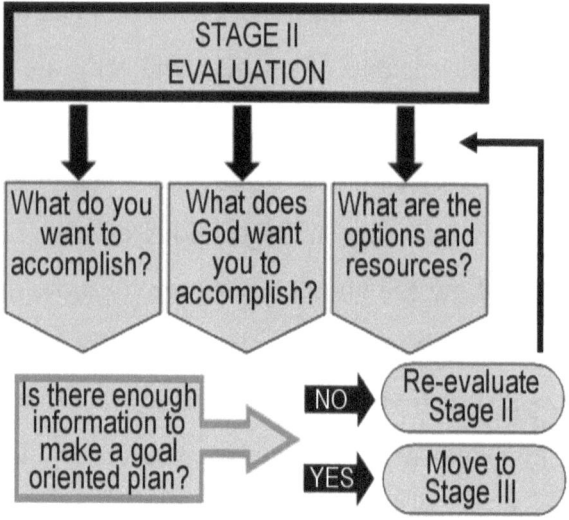

Now that you have maneuvered through these steps, help your client evaluate the question, "Is there enough information to make a goal-oriented and God-centered plan?" No? Try again. Yes? Move on.

8 SKILLED SPIRITUAL SUPPORTER MODEL STAGE III, IMPLEMENTATION

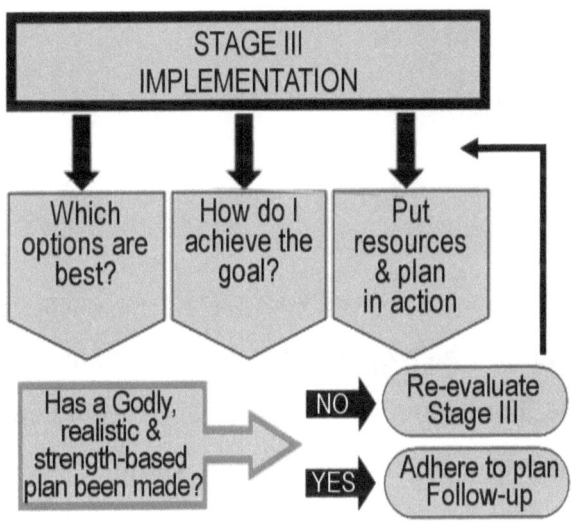

In this stage the client is actively putting his plan

into effect. They may need a lot of reassurance and encouragement. Remember, they may be stepping out their comfort zone, trying something new, or asking for help in ways they never have before. For many clients, this stage demonstrates great leaps of faith. You are modeling God's devotion to us by reinforcing your pleasure at their effort.

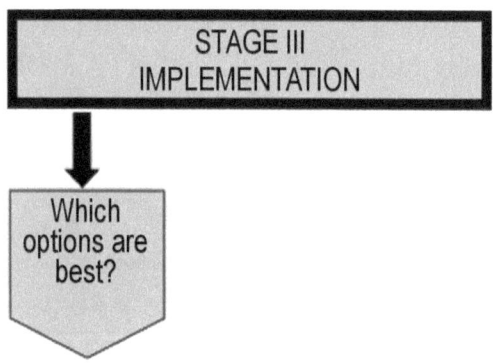

This step is where you guide your client into evaluating which options are the most realistic and viable. For example, while most of us would enjoy moving to a deserted island and starting over, for most of us, it is a profoundly unrealistic option. As you recall in Stage Three you led your client in a brainstorming session. They listed their personal strengths, their supporters, and potentially helpful community resources. Some of the options may not be feasible for a variety of reasons. Some options may require preparation or fore-planning before they can be implemented. Remember, you are trying to facilitate self-sufficiency, so here, you are simply reminding them to make their options work for them.

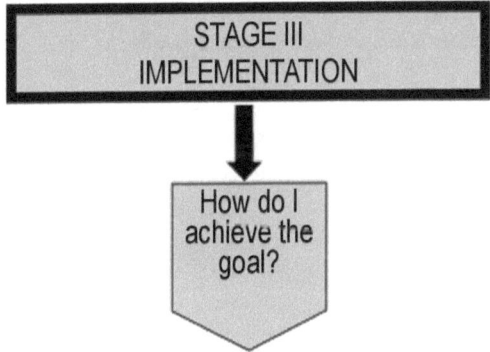

This is where you help your client review their strengths and resources to identify the plan. Back to Jane: you may recall that she listed job search resources as options. At this stage she makes her decisions and plans to visit online websites, local job fairs, and local career centers. Perhaps she needs transportation to job fairs or requires access to a computer. She may decide that she can ask her parents for rides to career centers which typically have online access available. Again, be mindful that your client is doing the problem solving here. You are guiding not directing.

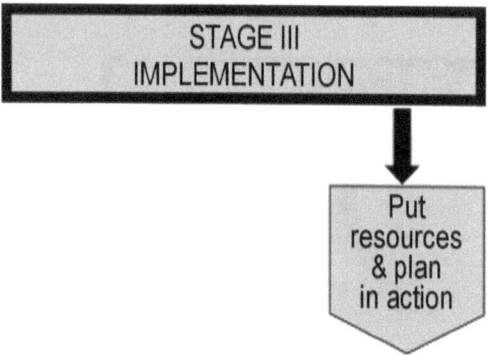

This can be the most rewarding step. Your client is now making her phone calls, or applying for jobs, or reaching out in her relationships. For some clients, their change will be immediate, for others change takes time. Perhaps they are rebuilding trust, perhaps they must wait for job call-backs. Help your client prayerfully seek peace while waiting for results.

Sadly this is also the step with the potential for the most failure. It is not easy to implement change. Even if we are miserable, sometimes leaving the familiar behind is frightening. Your greatest strength in this step as a Skilled Spiritual Supporter is to demonstrate over and over that you are proud of your client's effort and remind her of the blessings promised her by God for faithful adherence to His will for them.

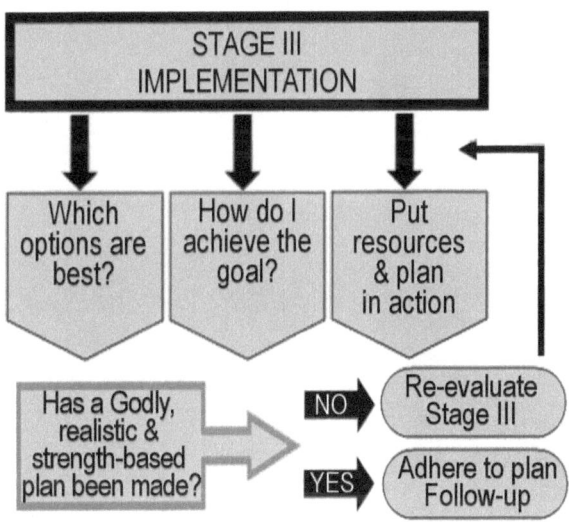

Now that your client has made his plan and implemented his plan, it is time to evaluate the effectiveness of the process. Has a Godly, realistic and strength-based plan been developed by the client and put into action by the client? No? Start by re-evaluating the options and the efficacy of implementing them. Yes? GREAT! Keep encouraging your client to continue seeking scriptural and prayerful support while they continue to work their plan.

9 SKILLED SPIRITUAL SUPPORTER MODEL STAGE IV, FOLLOW-UP

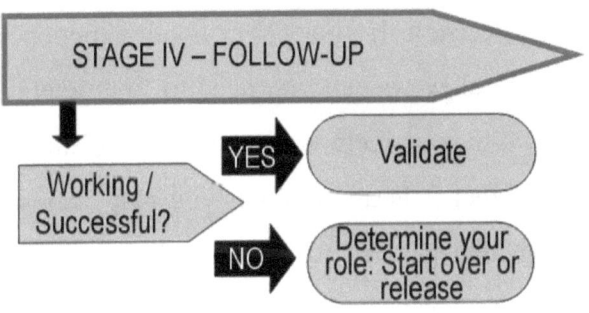

The timing on your follow up with your client will vary based on his original needs and his plan. Perhaps your client is already checking in with you, this means you are already aware of their progress. In some instances however, you will want to check in with him. For some scenarios, such as Jane's, 30-60 days is a good check in. You have given her time to apply for jobs and participate in interviews. Your follow up contact is simple. "Hi Jane, I'm checking back in on you. How is your plan coming?" Is she reporting success? Validate her, express pride and admiration with an emphasis on fostering her pride in herself, "Look what you accomplished!"

This is one of the toughest stages for you as a Skilled spiritual Supporter. If your client has not been as successful as they intended you must make a tough decision. If your client is not experiencing the results they wanted you need to first determine why. Did they actively work their plan? If they did, and you feel it is appropriate, you may choose to reengage the process with your client. This may mean going back to reassessing options, and it may mean reassessing the core issue. If they did not actively engage with their plan and intentions, you may need to consider releasing any sense of responsibility you may feel.

A therapeutic phrase we use often in the

industry is that 'you cannot work harder than your client.' This means that if your client is not doing his part to change his life, it is not your responsibility to make him change. It is important to be honest with dignity. For example, let's say Jane does not have a job at a 60 day check in. She reports she forgot to call her mom for a ride to the job fair and she says she "never got around to finishing her resume anyway." This is not a failed plan, it is failed implementation. I would encourage you to pray with Jane and let her hear you ask God to strengthen her resolve to work her plan. You will need to be clear with yourself, if you are going to start over, that is offer to help your client re-engage in solution-focused effort, or release your client.

FINAL NOTES

A friend from church approaches you and emotionally asks if you have time to talk. He or she reveals frustration at personal circumstances and asks you for advice. Now what?

> ➢ **Pray for clarity**
> ➢ **Work the model**
> ➢ **Remember to evaluate:**
> > ✓ **Safety of client and self**
> > ✓ **Scriptural soundness**
> > ✓ **Scope of skill required**
> > ✓ **Ethical considerations**

Clearly if your friend has an emergency those circumstances will dictate your next move. Otherwise, what is your role? How does God want you to respond? How can you help? Should you help? Working through the Skilled Spiritual Supporter Model will help you to answer those questions. Just remember to be mindful of scripture, safety, scope, and ethics.

Lastly, in a life where we are supporting others in times of grief or crisis, we can become overwhelmed. It is incredibly important that we stay grounded in the Bible and take care of ourselves. My final note to you is to encourage you to create a self-care plan for yourself. Use your plan to decompress from tough cases and keep yourself refreshed in God. You cannot serve water from an empty well.

"Above all else, guard you heart, for everything you do flows from it." Proverbs 4:23

ABOUT THE AUTHOR

Pastor Amy Halas Goff (BS, MS) is a teacher, speaker, ordained minister, and community chaplain with a heart for seeing families restored and individuals spiritually healed. She has supervised the development and implementation of counseling ministries and trained pastoral counselors and mentors throughout California. She is a proud wife, mom, and Grammy. Amy can be contacted directly for seminars, workshops, and support at courseworkgoff@gmail.com.